# THE ALAMO

# THE ALAMO

**DILLON PRESS**
New York

Maxwell Macmillan Canada
Toronto
Maxwell Macmillan International
New York   Oxford   Singapore   Sydney

*by Herma Silverstein*

**Photo Credits**
James Blank: pages 2-3, 12; The Alamo: pages 8, 11, 19, 24, 26, 31, 39, 44, 47, 50, 54, 55, 58, 59, 61, 62, and 64; The Bettmann Archive: pages 34, 38, and 42

**Library of Congress Cataloging-in Publication Data**
Silverstein, Herma.
   The Alamo / by Herma Silverstein.
      p.   cm. — (Places in American history)
   Includes bibliographical references and index.
   Summary: Describes the history behind and the events leading up to the famous battle between the Texans and Mexicans in 1836.
   ISBN 0-87518-502-9
1. Alamo (San Antonio, Tex.)—Siege, 1836—Juvenile literature. [1. Alamo (San Antonio, Tex.)—Siege.] I. Title. II. Series.
F390.S56 1992
976.4'03—dc20                                    91-42461

Dillon Press
Macmillan Publishing Company
866 Third Avenue
New York, NY 10022

Maxwell Macmillan Canada, Inc.
1200 Eglinton Avenue East
Suite 200
Don Mills, Ontario M3C 3N1

Macmillan Publishing Company is part of the Maxwell Communication Group of Companies.

First edition

Printed in the United States of America
10  9  8  7  6  5  4  3  2  1

# CONTENTS

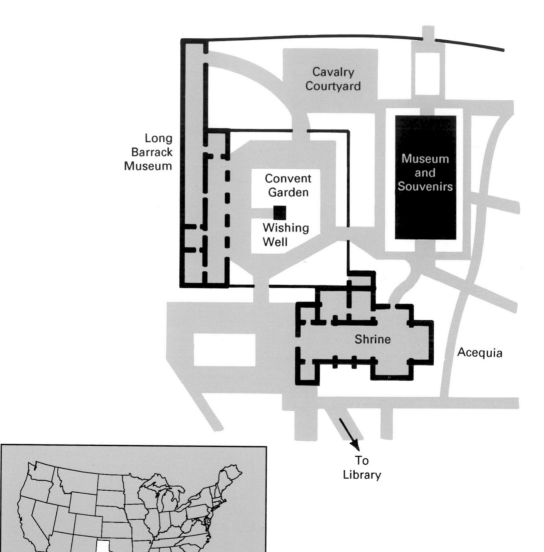

Cavalry
Courtyard

Long
Barrack
Museum

Convent
Garden

Wishing
Well

Museum
and
Souvenirs

Shrine

Acequia

To
Library

TEXAS

San Antonio

# CHAPTER 1

# THE MISSION ERA

The cannons had been silent for several hours. Colonel William Barret Travis stood on the hard-packed dirt in the center of the mission. The 189 men under his command, hollow eyed and weak from 12 days and nights of battle, waited for his instructions. A razor-sharp March wind blasted over the adobe walls, grazing the men's faces and ripping through their clothes.

Travis shivered. Then, his voice trembling, he addressed his men: The desperately awaited reinforcements were not coming. There would be no more food, guns, ammunition, or troops to help them defeat the 4,000-man Mexican army surrounding the Alamo. Unsheathing his sword,

he drew a line in the dirt. Any man who wanted to leave was free to go. Any man willing to stay should cross over the line. With such a death sentence hanging over his men, Colonel Travis did not expect to see many fighters cross the line. But, breaking the silence, a man in a raccoon cap joined Travis on the other side. He was David Crockett, a frontiersman and former congressman from Tennessee who, although having no obligation whatsoever to Texas, had volunteered to fight for the territory's independence. Then Colonel Jim Bowie, stricken with pneumonia, asked to be carried over in his cot. In scarcely a heartbeat, all the other men but one crossed the line. He was Lewis "Moses" Rose, who chose to leave the Alamo.

Committed to death, their ammunition almost gone, the Texas defenders took up their posts. If they had to die, at least they would make the Mexican victory a costly one. Colonel

*William Barret Travis leads his troops during the battle for the Alamo.*

Travis stood by his cannon. Davy Crockett led his Tennessee volunteers to the Long Barracks in the north wall. Jim Bowie lay on his cot in a room off the chapel, his famous knives at his side.

Also trapped in the death-wait were Captain Almeron Dickinson's wife, Susanna; their 15-month-old daughter, Angelina; Travis's aide, Joe; Gertrudis Navarro, 15, sister by adoption to Jim Bowie's wife; Juana Navarro Alsbury, Gertrudis's sister; her 18-month-old son, Alijo; Gregorio Esparza's wife, Ana; their four children: Enrique, Francisco, Manuel, and Maria; and two of the women's servants.

The silence of the cannons lasted about five hours. Some men dozed, while others spent their last minutes dreaming of wives and children they would never see again.

At 5:00 on the morning of Sunday, March 6, 1836, General Antonio Lopez de Santa Anna, commander of the Mexican army, ordered the

*Jim Bowie*

bugles to sound the "Deguello," Spanish for "to slit the throat." The men and women of the Alamo, hearing the Deguello, knew it meant that no life was to be spared. Santa Anna's army attacked the Alamo from all sides. For one and a half hours, the freezing dawn was split by the sounds of running feet, exploding cannons, screaming men, crackling rifles, and clashing swords. By 6:30 A.M., all 189 men of the Alamo were dead.

The Alamo still stands today, in the midst of the Texas city of San Antonio. Now a national historic landmark, the famous structure has had many different inhabitants and has served many purposes. But long before the Alamo was ever built, Native Americans occupied the land that is now Texas. In fact, the state of Texas got its name from a group of tribes of the Caddo Nation living southeast of San Antonio. These Native Americans called themselves *tejas*, meaning friends, which Spanish explorers translated into *Texas*.

*The Alamo today, in a photograph taken at night*

During the early 1600s, a Coahuiltecan village known as Yanaguana thrived on what is now the site of the Alamo. Soon Spanish conquistadores (a Spanish word for leaders or conquerors) began exploring and settling in the area. The Spanish would, in fact, control Mexico and the land that would later become Texas for some 20 years. In 1691, the explorer Domingo de Terán-Damian Manazanet camped on the banks of a river in what we now call Texas. Manazanet, who would later become the first governor of Spanish Texas, named the river San Antonio de Padua because, as he said in his diary, "we reached it on his [Saint Antonio's] day." Some 18 years later, two Spanish priests camped along the same river. Not knowing it already had a name, fathers Antonio Olivares and Isidro Espinosa decided to give the river a name. By a strange coincidence, they also chose to call it San Antonio de Padua!

Father Olivares came to work at this place on the San Antonio River. There, in 1718, a Catholic mission was built out of sticks and straw. It was named San Antonio de Valero after the viceroy of Mexico, the marquis de Valero (a viceroy is the governor who rules for a king). A fort, or *presidio*, named Presidio de Bexar, after Valero's brother, the duke of Bexar, was built nearby. A settlement, Villa de Bexar, was built in 1731. Four other missions, which still stand today, were built during this time. Their purposes were to convert Native Americans to Christianity, educate them, and help the Spanish remain powerful.

In 1724 the original Mission San Antonio de Valero was replaced by a second mission; it was later destroyed by a hurricane. In 1727 the Catholic church and the Spanish government agreed to be responsible for the building of a new, fortified mission, which could also be used for defense. A third mission was begun, to be "not more than two cannon shots away from the presidio," according to the requirements of the Spanish government. Surrounded by a high wall, the mission contained a chapel, a convent, and living quarters.

The architectural plan of all Spanish missions was the same. There was a plaza or yard surrounded by a wall, a stone chapel, a stone convent, and a row of rooms built into the walls to serve as living quarters for the priests. The Native Americans whom the priests were converting shared these living quarters. This wing would become famous as the Long Barracks during the Texas Revolution. In addition, other rooms housed working places where crafts such as blacksmithing and tanning could be practiced. A ditch provided water from the San Antonio River.

The first stone church of the mission was begun in 1744. By 1756 the church had collapsed owing to poor construction. Two years later, the church that still stands today was started, with the date 1758 inscribed above the door. This church, however, was never fully completed during the Alamo's mission days.

In 1793, a series of epidemics wiped out most of the Texas missions. The mission that would later be named the Alamo, including its unfinished chapel, was inhabited only by the remaining Native Americans. The Alamo's 75 years as a mission had come to an end.

# CHAPTER 2

# A CALL TO ARMS

By 1800 the mission that would be known as the Alamo was completely deserted. Meanwhile, in Mexico, armed rebellions broke out between native Mexicans and the Spanish, who had ruled Mexico for almost 300 years. The Spanish transferred cavalry from El Alamo, Mexico, to Bexar to protect the region from invasion by native Mexicans. The cavalry occupied the Mission San Antonio de Valero, using it as headquarters and barracks. The religious mission had now become a military outpost.

The soldiers, lonely for their homes in El Alamo (which means "cottonwood trees" in

*Downtown San Antonio has grown up around the Alamo*

Spanish), found a pleasant reminder of their Mexican village in the cottonwood trees growing beside the San Antonio River. Eventually the Spanish government changed the name of San Antonio de Valero to the name of their village, Pueblo del Alamo. The mission has been known as the Alamo ever since.

Resistance to Spanish rule in Mexico intensified between 1810 and 1817. The Spanish government, determined to stop the rebellions, sent an expedition commanded by a Mexican-born Spanish officer, Augustin de Iturbide, against the native Mexicans. However, instead of crushing the native Mexican rebellion, Iturbide joined the rebels as their leader and crushed the Spanish cavalry. By September 1821, the Spanish were gone. Mexico was declared an independent country, and Spain's former provinces, including Texas, became Mexican provinces. In 1822 Iturbide had himself proclaimed Emperor

Augustin I of Mexico.

The end of Spanish rule over Mexico did not end Mexico's problems. The Mexican people felt they had gained independence from Spain only to be put under the rule of an emperor. Iturbide was just as cruel as the Spanish viceroys had been. The Mexicans overthrew Iturbide in 1823, and a year later Mexico became a republic. This meant that Mexico was ruled by someone who was not a king. Guadalupe Victoria was elected Mexico's first president. Still, the country sizzled with plots and counterplots, as army officers schemed against one another and President Victoria for power.

During the bitter fighting, no one paid attention to Mexico's northern province of Texas. There, colonists from the United States were living on land granted by Mexico. They had come filled with the spirit of independence granted by the American Constitution. The movement of

American colonists into Texas disturbed Mexico. Would the Americans try to take over Texas?

To make sure this did not happen, the Mexican government prohibited additional land grants to Americans. The ban enraged Americans already settled in the province of Texas. Also annoying to the Mexican government was the fact that France claimed the Texas territory as theirs. French explorer Robert Cavalier Sieur de La Salle had led expeditions into the area in 1685. The Mexicans claimed France had never sent officials to govern the territory and therefore had no legal rights to Texas.

Then, when Emperor Napoleon Bonaparte of France sold the Louisiana Territory to the United States in 1803, the United States claimed Texas was French. Thus Texas now belonged to the United States, purchased along with Louisiana. However, like France, the United States did little to govern Texas. Instead adventurous Americans were sent to settle the land. By 1830 there were 30,000 American settlers in Texas.

One of the Mexican army officers eager to snatch Mexico for himself was a ruthless man who would become legendary as the general who defeated the men of the Alamo. This man was Antonio Lopez de Santa Anna. He had himself declared president of Mexico in 1833. Two years later he seized all government powers, a move that triggered a series of events that would lead to 189 men giving up their lives at the Alamo.

American colonists were already angry with Santa Anna for imprisoning Stephen F. Austin, a leading colonist in Texas. Two years earlier Santa Anna had ordered the land of Texas to be combined with the Mexican state of Coahuila, causing Texans to lose a voice in Mexican affairs. Austin petitioned Mexico to restore Texas to Mexican statehood. "War is our only resource," Austin wrote on September 19, 1835. "There is

no other remedy but to defend our rights, our country, ourselves by force of arms." Austin's plea to defend Texans' rights united the Texan-Hispanic community against Mexico and especially against Santa Anna.

Much of the revolutionary activity to separate Texas from Mexico centered around the settlement of Bexar, which was now inside the Mexican state of Coahuila owing to Santa Anna's annexation. Santa Anna sent 1,200 Mexican troops to occupy Bexar. He appointed his brother-in-law, General Martin Perfecto de Cos, leader of the troops, and ordered anyone who opposed him arrested. In addition, all Texans who had lived in Bexar less than five years were ordered to return to the United States.

De Cos stationed his troops in the vacant Alamo. The army removed the Alamo chapel's roof and piled the debris against the east wall, forming a ramp on which to haul up their

*General Santa Anna*

cannons. On October 2, 1835, at the town of
Gonzales, about 65 miles (105 kilometers) east of
Bexar, the Mexican army demanded that Texans
in the area surrender their only cannon. "Come
and get it," the angry Texans responded, then fired
a cannon shot. The Texas Revolution had begun.

American volunteers stormed into the town
of Gonzales near Bexar. Some of the units were
commanded by Stephen F. Austin, who had been
released from prison. (The Mexican government
accused him of trying to unite Texas with the
United States. Although Austin was in prison for
two years, he never received a trial.) They were
joined by the New Orleans Greys, a U.S. volunteer force that had marched all the way from
New Orleans to reinforce the Texas army.

Meanwhile, on November 7, 1835, 57 Texans
wrote a Declaration of Causes explaining why
they were going to war against Mexico. The
document stated that Santa Anna had over-

*General de Cos*

thrown the federal institutions of Mexico and thus wiped out any mutual understandings between Texas and the Mexican confederacy. The Texans were defending their liberties and those of the federal constitution of Mexico. Among the signers was Sam Houston, who would become the first president of the Republic of Texas.

On December 5, 300 men of the army of Texas attacked de Cos's troops in Bexar and at the Alamo. Three days later de Cos surrendered, agreeing never to fight Texans again. He would not keep his promise.

The Alamo had been a Catholic mission, Spanish military headquarters, and then a Mexican stronghold. Now it was a Texas garrison. What used to be the Alamo's convent became a lodging for soldiers called the Long Barracks. The upper floor became the garrison hospital.

In Mexico, General Santa Anna, enraged by the defeat of de Cos, took command of a 4,000-

man army and headed to Bexar. He was out for revenge against the Texans. Arriving on February 23, 1836, Santa Anna immediately ordered a red flag hoisted atop the San Fernando Church. It was a signal to the Texans to surrender or be killed.

The Texans barricaded themselves inside the Alamo. When Colonel Travis saw the red flag, he fired a single cannon shot at the Mexicans—his response to Santa Anna's ultimatum. There would be no surrender.

# CHAPTER 3

# THE SIEGE BEGINS

The Alamo was under the joint command of Colonel William Barret Travis, a 27-year-old lawyer, and Colonel James Bowie, a famous frontiersman and a Bexar resident. Also inside the Alamo were a company of Tennessee volunteers led by Bowie and a three-term congressman from Tennessee, David Crockett. Crockett told the residents of Bexar, "I have come to aid you all that I can in your noble cause . . . and all the honor I desire is that of defending . . . the liberties of our common country."

The joint command did not last long, as Bowie became fatally ill with pneumonia and had to remain in his quarters. The command now fell solely to Travis. On February 16, he sent his boyhood friend from South Carolina, James Bonham, to Goliad, a town 90 miles (145 kilometers) southeast of San Antonio, to ask for reinforcements.

There, Colonel James W. Fannin was temporary head of the Texas army. Bonham pleaded with Fannin for troops, telling him of Santa Anna's large army, and assured Fannin that his troops could still get through to the Alamo if they hurried. Fannin refused, and Bonham delivered the bad news to Travis.

On February 23 and again on February 29, Travis sent scouts to beg Fannin for help. By March 1 they had not returned. The men at the Alamo were desperate for news of what Fannin was doing with his army of 500 volunteers. Colonel Fannin had retreated to Goliad after abandoning an attack on the city of Matamoros, where a Mexican army of over 1,000 men had awaited him.

In Goliad, Fannin drilled his army—an army he would never use. As he had abandoned the attack at Matamoros, Fannin now abandoned the men at the Alamo, putting off the decision about sending reinforcements. Instead, he wrote letters to the newly formed Acting Committee at the Texas Constitutional Convention for instructions. On February 5, when another courier arrived in Goliad, Fannin realized that for his own reputation's sake he'd better try to stop the siege at the Alamo. He ordered his troops to move out on the 26th.

Yet they did not leave until two days later, on the 28th. The men had little ammunition and were inadequately clothed for the cold Texas weather. As they crossed the San Antonio River, three wagons broke down. Fannin left the wagons there "to keep the powder dry," while his troops crossed. No fodder had been brought to feed the oxen pulling the wagons, and they were turned loose to graze. By the next morning the oxen were gone. Fannin's men had only their

own rounds of ammunition with which to fight, while the food and major ammunition, with no animals to pull the wagons across, remained on the other side of the river.

While Fannin floundered, five Texans who had escaped from the battle with the Mexicans at Matamoros reached Fannin. They reported that Mexican troops were headed for Goliad. With his troops undersupplied and Santa Anna's huge army closing in on the Alamo, Fannin decided to return to Goliad.

At the Alamo, Travis grew even more desperate. He wrote a plea for reinforcements on February 24, 1836:

> To the people of Texas & all Americans in the world. Fellow citizens and compatriots. I am besieged by a thousand or more of the Mexicans under Santa Anna————I have sustained a continual bombardment &

*The battle for the Alamo begins.*

cannonade for 24 hours & have not lost a man————The enemy has demanded a surrender at discretion, otherwise the garrison is to be put to the sword if the fort is taken————I have answered the demand with a cannon shot, & our flag still waves proudly from the walls————I shall never surrender or retreat. Then, I call you in the name of liberty, of patriotism & everything dear to the American character, to come to our aid with all dispatch————the enemy is receiving reinforcements daily & will no doubt increase to three or four thousand in four or five days. If this call is neglected, I am determined to sustain myself as long as possible & die like a soldier who never forgets what is due to his own honor & that of his country. Victory or death. Lieutenant Colonel William Barret Travis, Commander.

In response to Travis's plea for reinforcements,

32 volunteers from Gonzales sneaked into the Alamo, raising hopes for victory. Travis sent his friend Bonham out again on February 27 to ask Fannin for help. Bonham returned on March 3. With Mexican gunfire directed at him, Bonham leaned over the side of his horse and rode through the Alamo gates. His report was short. Fannin would send no help.

Travis made one last effort to get help. He wrote a letter to governor of Texas Henry Smith and the commander-in-chief of the Texas army, General Sam Houston. He sent expert scout John W. Smith to deliver the plea.

On March 2, the day before Travis wrote this letter, 57 delegates from 23 Texas towns adopted a declaration of independence. But the men in the Alamo never learned about it and consequently never knew they were fighting for the Republic of Texas.

Santa Anna's soldiers attacked the Alamo for

*The last stand*

*A vest believed to have been worn by Davy Crockett during the battle for the Alamo.*

12 straight days, during which the Texas defenders never slept and hardly ate. They watched in horror as the Mexicans moved closer and closer to the Alamo walls. Texas cannons returned the fire, tearing apart the enemy's lines.

Occasionally, during a lull in the cannon roar, the Mexicans were puzzled by the shrill, sad tones of a bagpipe and the scratchy notes of a fiddle floating through the air. The fiddler was Davy Crockett, and the piper was John McGregor, a Scotsman who had settled in Texas and joined the fight for freedom. Then, on the evening of March 5, the cannons stopped. Silence fell over the Alamo.

# CHAPTER 4

# THE BATTLE OF THE ALAMO

Legend says that during the lull, Colonel Travis drew a line in the dirt with his sword, ordering all men willing to stay to cross over the line. All but one of the defenders crossed over. All through the night of March 5 and the morning of March 6, the Texas defenders waited for death.

It arrived at 5:00 A.M. A column of Mexican soldiers charged the Alamo carrying ladders. The Texans mowed them down with rifle fire as they reached the top of the walls. From debris inside the chapel, the Texans made a ramp to run a cannon up to the top of the walls. Travis manned the 12-pound (5.5 kilogram) cannon on the northwest corner.

Davy Crockett and his men stationed themselves on the southeast side of the courtyard, guarding the wall that ran from the chapel to the south wall. Jim Bonham stood atop the chapel, commanding three cannons. Fatally ill but armed, Jim Bowie lay on his cot in the southwest corner of the chapel. Davy Crockett had given him several loaded pistols. The woman and children hid nearby in the chapel.

The Texans rallied at the successful slaughter of the first soldiers of Santa Anna's trying to scale the walls. If the Texans could defeat another column, Santa Anna might stop the assault. So effective was the barrage of musket balls against the Mexicans that two Mexican commanders disobeyed orders and, instead of remaining on the south side, marched toward

*A lantern slide shows another view of the fighting*

*One of the knives used during the battle, the so-called Bowie knife was named after Jim Bowie.*

the western wall. The column on the east went around to the north side. These shifts in position made the Texas cannons pointing south and east useless. The Texans had no choice but to stand on top of the walls and fire, where they were shot down instantly.

Yet despite the new arrangement of Mexican troops, the Texans succeeded in repulsing the second attack, picking the Mexicans off the tops of the ladders so that they tumbled down onto the men below. However, the third assault on the walls was more than the Texans could fend off. The Mexican army poured over the northeast wall. Outnumbered and outweaponed, the defenders nevertheless hung on until one by one they were slaughtered by the Mexican army.

They fought hand-to-hand with pistols, rifle butts, knives, bayonets, sticks, and their fists. Davy Crockett was shot in his right arm and began firing with his left until his gun barrel was broken off. Then he fought with his knife.

The Mexicans took over the cannons abandoned by fallen Texans and turned them on the mission, ripping out door after door, storming the rooms, and killing those inside with their bayonets. Susanna Dickinson and the other women, children, and servants were not harmed but were sent to Santa Anna's headquarters, an adobe house on the street leading south from the Alamo. Eventually they were released.

Colonel Travis may have been the first man killed at the Alamo. He was shot in the head and fell over his cannon. Yet he managed to muster enough strength to sit up once, when General Mora of the Mexican army rushed him with a bayonet. With his last breath, Travis lunged and sank his sword into the general. Dying, the general stabbed Travis, and the two men fell dead together. Travis's servant Joe, who witnessed the incident while hiding in one of the rooms, said

*The battle rages on*

Travis's last words were, "Don't surrender, boys."

Now the Mexicans turned to the Long Barracks and the chapel. The same two-story building that had been the scene of quiet prayers would now become the scene of ruthless massacre. The Texans barricaded the doors with bearskins and cowhides stretched on poles, the inner cavities of the hides stuffed with earth. Behind this clever barricade the Texans at first fired at the enemy with ease, stacking up dead in large numbers as the Mexicans tried to enter. But their bravery was not enough to repel the great number of Mexican troops. Room after room fell to the invaders.

Davy Crockett stood in a stretch of ground between the chapel and the south wall. He had been assigned four cannons. "Just give me my place to defend," he told Travis, "and me and my Tennessee boys will hold it." When the firing was over, Crockett and his men were found at their posts. In his hand was "Old Betsy," his favorite rifle. The greatest number of enemy dead is said to have been found around Crockett's body. Santa Anna's cook said a soldier lay across Crockett, his knife buried to the hilt in the man's chest.

The remaining Texans withdrew into the chapel. The Mexican troops met stubborn resistance from Bonham and his men, including Mrs. Dickinson's husband, Almeron. Although the Texans were equipped with a cannon, there were no more musket balls left to fire. The men plugged their guns with rocks, cast iron, and broken pieces of chain. A Mexican officer aimed a force of muskets on the men. Bonham fell, followed by the other cannoneers.

Now Jim Bowie waited in the small baptistry in the southwest corner of the Alamo, the pistols left by Davy Crockett at his side. When the Mexicans burst in, they thought Bowie was a ghost because he was so pale and his body was

*A long-distance view of the battle*

so emaciated. But Bowie was not yet dead. With tremendous effort he fired at the enemy, holding his knife ready for those who came near. When at last his ammunition ran out, Mexican bodies filled the doorway and surrounded the cot where the dead Bowie lay. By 6:30 A.M., the 189 defenders of the Alamo lay dead.

# CHAPTER 5

# "REMEMBER THE ALAMO!"

**A**lthough the heroes of the Alamo were dead, the fighting continued. A testimony by Felix Nunez, one of Santa Anna's men, said that in the darkness and in the excitement of victory, the Mexican soldiers "became uncontrollable and fell to killing one another, not being able to distinguish friend from foe." Enrique Esparza, one of the children in the Alamo, reported that the enemy "for fully a quarter of an hour kept firing at the dead men after all the defenders had been slain and their corpses were lying still."

In the courtyard, there were more than 500 bodies, many huddled together, holding a hand to a throat or a sword to a chest. Francis Antonio Ruiz, the mayor of Bexar, described the scene: "On the north battery of the fortress lay the lifeless body of Colonel Travis on the gun carriage, shot only in the forehead. Toward the west, and in the small fort opposite the city, we found the body of Colonel Crockett. . . ."

Six hundred Mexican soldiers were killed in the battle. Santa Anna ordered the face of every dead man wiped clean of grime so that he could tell the Mexicans from the Texans. Then he ordered the Texans' bodies burned. The corpses were stacked into a funeral pyre, and a torch was lit.

Weeks later, Juan Seguin, a Texas soldier who had been sent to seek aid from Fannin, returned to the Alamo and gathered the piles of ashes into a coffin. With the names Travis, Bowie, and Crockett engraved on the lid, he carried the

*"Remember the Alamo!"*

coffin to the Church of San Fernando for burial, the same church where Santa Anna had raised his red flag on the first day of the battle.

The bloody fighting between Mexico and Texas continued for two more battles. First Santa Anna attacked Goliad. On March 19, he again defeated the Texans, taking 300 prisoners, including Colonel Fannin. All were executed.

Next Santa Anna went after Texans at San Jacinto, on the site of present-day Houston. On April 21, 1836, General Sam Houston and 783 Texans surprised the 1,500 advance men of Santa Anna's army. Cutting off any escape route by blowing up a bridge, Houston and his men fell upon the Mexicans with a vengeance.

"Remember the Alamo!" "Remember Goliad!" the Texans screamed as they charged.

Eighteen minutes later, 630 Mexicans lay dead. The rest were taken prisoner, among them Santa Anna. Only nine Texans were killed. The

Battle of San Jacinto ended the war for Texas independence. The Republic of Texas was a reality.

The United States immediately recognized Texas, but it was not until 1848 that the Mexicans gave Texas recognition. On December 29, 1845, Texas gave up its independence once more to join the United States as America's 28th state. Because Texas is the only state that was ever a republic, it is also the only state allowed to raise its state flag as high as the American flag.

General Santa Anna was set free after signing the treaty making Texas a state, then booted out of Mexico for losing Texas. When Mexico and the United States went to war in 1846 over a territorial dispute, Santa Anna returned to command the Mexican army. Defeated three times, at Buena Vista, Cerro Gordo, and Capultepec, Santa Anna fled the country. In 1874, nearly 80 years old, he returned to Mexico City, where he died a poor and broken man.

The fate of the Alamo in 1836 was uncertain. The Catholic church wanted the Alamo returned to them. In 1842 their wish was granted, but the church was unable to restore the Alamo as a place of worship.

In 1847, the church rented the Alamo to the U.S. government as a supply depot. Thanks to American soldiers, in 1849 the chapel finally had a complete roof. When the Civil War (1861–1865) broke out, Confederate forces occupied San Antonio and used the Alamo as a garrison. After the war, the Alamo was returned to the U.S. army, which again used it as a supply depot until 1876, when the army moved to Fort Sam Houston in San Antonio.

Now the Catholic church needed a new tenant. A merchant, Honore Grenet, bought the Long Barracks in 1877 and turned it into a general store, with castlelike towers. The Alamo was now called Grenet's Palace. He used the

*The Alamo about 1847. At this time the building was used as a supply depot.*

*By the 1860s the Alamo was occupied by the U.S. Army and used as a garrison.*

Alamo chapel as a warehouse for his merchandise. Grenet's Palace, the Alamo Beer Garden, Saloon and Restaurant, and the city meat market now occupied the Alamo.

Texans worried that the Alamo was becoming undignified. A campaign to restore the mission and make it a national shrine began in 1883. By 1885 Texas turned the chapel over to the city of San Antonio. When Honore Grenet died, his "Palace" was sold to men who turned it into a department store called Hugo & Schmeltzer. In 1903 the department store put up a FOR SALE sign, looking for someone who might turn the property into a hotel.

Texans rallied to keep the site as a historic monument. The Daughters of the Republic of Texas, formed in 1891 to preserve the history of Texas independence, tried to raise money to restore the Alamo. They were unsuccessful, and hope of making the Alamo into a monument faded.

*The Alamo during its life as a department store*

Then, in 1904, Clara Driscoll, whose grandfathers had fought at San Jacinto, bought the property and a year later gave it to the state of Texas.

The state returned to Mrs. Driscoll all the money she had invested and appointed the Daughters of the Republic of Texas guardians. By agreement, they would provide money to maintain the Alamo as a shrine of Texas liberty without seeking funds from the state of Texas. In 1960 the Alamo was declared a national historic landmark by the United States government.

There is no admission fee charged to visit the Alamo, and no formal tours are given. Rather, visitors are free to roam the chapel, the only building remaining of the original mission, on their own. In the Long Barracks Museum, where Catholic priests lived during the mission period, are artifacts from the Alamo heroes. Guns, uniforms, letters, and eating utensils, as well as historical portraits, documents, and coins are on display.

*Work begins on the Alamo in an effort to turn it into the monument it has become today.*

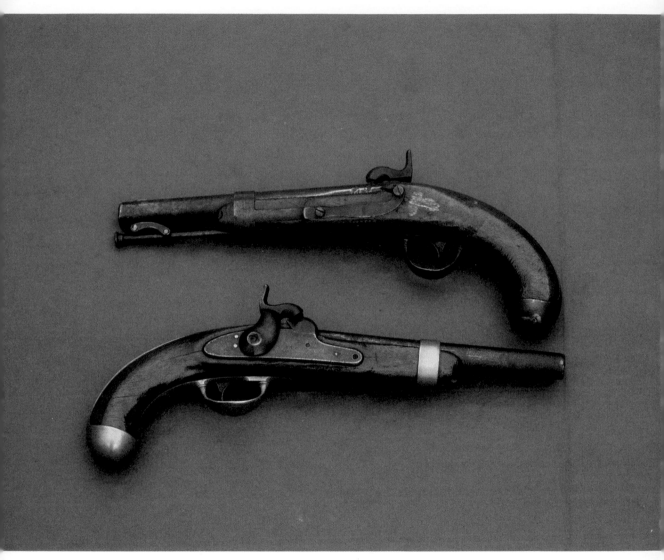

*These percussion cap pistols, used during the battle,*
*are on display today.*

In addition, the north side of the gardens houses the Texas Historical Research Library of the Daughters of the Republic of Texas, containing books, maps, documents, art works, and other memorabilia of Texas history spanning four centuries.

Although the battle at San Jacinto was the one that ended Mexican rule over Texas, it is the battle of the Alamo that is remembered most. Since that Sunday in March of 1836, the Alamo has become a shrine to the people of Texas and a reminder to the people of America of the value of freedom as they recall the 189 men who gave their lives for Texas's freedom.

Stand in the courtyard where Davy Crockett fell and in the baptistry where James Bowie fought from his bed. Use your imagination to bring history to life. Perhaps you can see the heroes firing their rifles over the adobe walls or hear the ancient cannons exploding while ghosts of the past shout, "Remember the Alamo!"

# Visitor Information

**Hours:**
Monday-Saturday: 9:00 A.M. to 5:30 P.M.
Sunday: 10:00 A.M. to 5:30 P.M.          Closed: December 24-25

**Admission:**
Free. The Daughters of the Republic of Texas relies solely on donations and proceeds from the gift shop for maintenance of Alamo Complex.

**Tours & Services:**
Scheduled history talks are as follows: Monday-Saturday: first one starts at 9:15 A.M., then there is one every 45 minutes until 11:30 A.M. They resume at 1:00 P.M. and end at 4:45 P.M. Sunday: first one starts at 10:15 A.M. and then follows the same schedule as above for Monday-Saturday.

Special talks for tour groups may be arranged by calling 512-225-1391 for reservations.

A 15-minute documentary video is shown continuously in the Long Barrack Museum.

Daughters of the Republic of Texas History Research Library (closed Sundays).

**Special Events:**
Texas Independence Day and Texas Flag Day Celebration—March 2.
Alamo Memorial Service—March 6.
Pilgrimage to the Alamo—Monday, the week of April 21.

Photographic policy: Out of respect for the 189 Alamo heroes who gave their lives for freedom, you are asked not to take photographs of any kind while inside the buildings of the Alamo Complex.

**Additional Information may be obtained from:**

The Alamo
300 Alamo Plaza
San Antonio, TX 78299
(512) 225-1391
          or

The Alamo Visitor's Information Center
317 Alamo Street
(right across from the Alamo)
San Antonio, TX 78299
(512) 299-8155 or (800) 447-3372

# The Alamo: A Historical Time Line

**1691**    Spanish expedition led by Domingo de Terán-Damian Manazanet visits present-day San Antonio area.

**1718**    Spanish mission, San Antonio de Valero, built on west bank of San Antonio River.

**1724**    Second mission replaces San Antonio de Valero (later destroyed by a hurricane).

**1727**    Third Spanish mission built, with chapel, convent, and living quarters.

**1793**    San Antonio de Valero abandoned as a mission; inhabited by Native Americans.

**1801**    Spanish cavalry occupies San Antonio de Valero; renamed Pueblo de Alamo.

**1821**    Mexico wins independence from Spain (including land that is now Texas).

**Oct. 2, 1835**    The first battle of the Texas Revolution begins at Gonzales.

**Oct. 9, 1835**    Mexican General de Cos occupies the Alamo and San Antonio de Bexar.

**Dec. 5, 1835**    The Battle of Bexar begins; General de Cos eventually surrenders the Alamo and San Antonio de Bexar.

FEB. 23, 1836    Santa Anna's army arrives in San Antonio de Bexar; Texans move into the Alamo.

MAR. 1, 1836    Thirty-two volunteer reinforcements join the Alamo.

MAR. 2, 1836    Texas declares independence from Mexico.

MAR. 6, 1836    The Alamo falls.

MAR. 27, 1836    Colonel James Fannin and 400 Texans slain at Goliad.

APR. 21, 1836    General Sam Houston and Texans defeat Santa Anna at the Battle of San Jacinto, ending the Texas Revolution.

MAY 14, 1836    The Treaty of Velasco recognizes Texas as an independent republic.

1845    Republic of Texas becomes America's 28th state.

1847    The Catholic church rents the Alamo to the U.S. government for military use.

1861    The Alamo becomes a Confederate garrison during the Civil War.

1864    The U.S. army again leases the Alamo.

**1876**   Honore Grenet, a merchant, buys part of the Alamo and erects "Grenet's Palace."

**1883**   The state of Texas buys the Alamo chapel.

**1885**   Texas gives Alamo chapel to city of San Antonio; Grenet's Palace sold to department store company.

**1904**   Clara Driscoll buys the Alamo.

**1905**   Clara Driscoll gives the Alamo to the state of Texas.

**1960**   The Alamo is declared a national historic landmark.

# FOR FURTHER READING

De Zavala, Adina. *The Alamo*. San Antonio: The Naylor Company, Texas, 1956.

Fisher, Leonard Everett. *The Alamo*. New York: Holiday House, 1987.

Jakes, John. *Susanna of the Alamo: A True Story*. New York: Harcourt Brace Jovanovich, 1986.

Myers, John. *The Alamo*. New York: E.P. Dutton, 1948.

Tinkle, Lon. *Thirteen Days to Glory*. New York: McGraw-Hill, 1958.

Warren, Robert Penn. *Remember the Alamo!* New York: Random House, 1958.

# INDEX

**PROSPECT FREE LIBRARY**
915 Trenton Falls St.
Prospect, NY 13435
(315) 896-2736

DEMCO